HANS KOTTER

NEW YORK
DE BUCK GALLERY

IN THE DEEP RAPTURE OF LIGHT AND COLOR

"Art is nothing but the light of nature" *Goethe*

Hans Kotter is an expert when it comes to colors and light. His main interest during his study of painting lay with color compositions, handling plane areas and structure, and color and form. At the end of the 1990s, he began to concentrate more and more on the medium of photography. Devising his own experimental set-ups, he devoted himself to the study of light and its segmentation into color spectra. The visualization and aesthetic staging of light refraction and color compositions of great virtuosity have been part of Kotter's basic repertoire of works since then:

"There is no other element with such a lasting impact on life on our planet as light. Light fascinates me in a huge variety of ways and I have investigated the medium of light, with its composition, physical contexts, colors, perception and cultural history for many years. The experiences and insights resulting from this investigation are later implemented in my works."

It is the playful treatment of a wide range of materials such as oil, water, acrylic glass, stainless steel, chrome etc. and their effects in relation to light and color which fascinates Hans Kotter and inspires him to try out new forms of expression continually. This diversity in the handling of materials is revealed in his works' great power of expression and variety.

The abstraction of color and light creates diffuse landscapes, the illusion of distance, mysterious waves, the impression of water, shimmering heat or the finest of fabrics, which seem to glide across the picture surface in undulating folds. The apparent materiality of these unmanipulated photographs of the immaterial – of light and colur – points to their origins in painting, yet at the same time they document physical processes. The incredible degree of beauty, opulence, brilliance and simultaneous mystery with which natural scientific insights can be manifest in art is quite remarkable.

The artist's treatment of color plays a key role in all this. Hans Kotter employs his profound knowledge of colors and *their very different effects in relation to light conditions and proximity to other colors* to relate them to each other systematically yet intuitively, so creating harmonies as well as extremely exciting contrasts.

The series of works *color codes* is evidence of this approach: *color codes* are light objects, the vertical colored structure of which illuminates ever fresh combinations of colors with endless variety. At first glance, these photographic collages, which are reminiscent of barcodes, create an effect using minimal aesthetics, unfolding a diverse play of color on the basis of LED lighting technology. A large number of optical and aesthetic impulses are created by changes in coloration; the codes appear to be moving slowly due to the changing color spectra. Even the surrounding wall space and the room itself cannot remain unaffected by this choreography of light and color.

Indeed, the room always plays an important part in Hans Kotter's installation works. Light is brought into play in a subtle way, for example, as a blue line: the cubature of the room disappears into the darkness, reduced to its contour lines. This abstraction of three-dimensional space certainly causes many details to disappear, but other elementary spatial information is manifest more clearly as a direct consequence. Three-dimensional compositions with fluorescent tubing and illuminated objects immerse different rooms into changing currents of light, and the viewer experiences a roller-coaster ride of sensory impressions and emotions.

In his latest works, the so-called "Tunnels", Hans Kotter is concerned with an illusion of space: in newly developed light objects consisting of filigree, reflecting glass volumes that generate a special aura of their own due to their superior material quality and precision, the approaching viewer is compelled by a mysterious and forceful attraction, which gradually develops into a deep rapture. As if by magic, the reflecting surfaces of the light object are transformed – when the source of light at the object's centre is switched on – into an enchanting tunnel of colors, the end of which is unforeseeable, and which – as in Alice in Wonderland – offers us apparently infinite freedom to develop our fantasies and imagination.

The tunnel pointing into infinity, whether curving or straight, is a phenomenon that appears so realistic one would like to extend one's hand into it; one is overcome by an irresistible attraction. But it is a game with illusion, with the apparently endless, constantly surprising and astonishing ways to stage light and color artistically. This extremely aesthetic and simultaneously mysterious interplay of reflecting surfaces and endless color compositions propels the viewer into a rapture of color and depth from which he has no desire to recover quickly, thanks to Hans Kotter!

ANNETT ZINSMEISTER

COLOUR CODE

2011

polished stainless steel light box, slide on Plexiglas, color-changing LED lights, and remote control

78 3/4 x 5 1/8 x 5 1/8 in

200 x 13 x 13 cm

DIFFUSION, CONCENTRATION, REFLECTION. INTUITIVE INSIGHT IN THE WORK OF HANS KOTTER

'Art that impresses the eye' is a heading that suits the latest works by Hans Kotter: cheerfully colorful three-dimensional and wall-mounted objects, and forms combining mirrors and light in wall-boxes all define the overall spatial context with their sensitively selected placement. At first glance, the compact exhibits with their bright colors and visual illusions suggest cheerfulness and innocence, making the dismal concrete surroundings of many an office building appear in a different light. But a second look reveals a deeper, meaningful dimension, which promises a profound 'illumination' full of insight.

Points of light arranged in a ring within a reflecting wall-box shine with absolute technical perfection, as can be seen in the work 'down under' (2011). Submerged in bluish or reddish light, the configurations of lights and mirrors develop a more intense atmospheric aura. The eye wanders rather disquieted through the objects' suggested depth, constantly attempting to find some visual hold. With a wry smile, Kotter highlights the inadequacy of the human perceptual apparatus, our eyes happily joining in his receptive game of lively 'conversation'. The tunnel formation of these points of light, however, causes the viewer's attention to wander away from the factual to the metaphorical dimension: in Kotter's works the well-known concept of tunnel vision, used to criticize a narrowing of perception and one's limited interpretation of key contexts, is extended into the infinity of three dimensions. Closure and opening thus become vital metaphors, not only in this single work but also from the artist's most recent creative phase.

From this perspective, Kotter goes a stage further than the aesthetically related innovations of the previous generation, particularly associated with the name Victor Vasarely and with Op Art. Vasarely's interest lay in illusionist effects, which he attempted to achieve by means of colors, forms and lines; he aimed, therefore, at irritations of vision, at immediacy in the contemplation of art, and ultimately at aesthetics that required no prior knowledge. But Kotter, who claims to see himself within a line of tradition from Vasarely, extends the field of visual irritation. While Vasarely, still entirely in the spirit of Minimal Art, had wished to ban meaning from art and employed his formal aesthetics as a pointer to the limitations of human perception, the semantic and therefore the narrative return in Kotter's work – which is characteristic, among other things, of the post-modern generation.

The several-part photographic works entitled 'Cliffs' or 'Chromatic Plants' (2009-2011) convey a disturbing impression. Their powerful colors form strange configurations, which appear indeterminate: are they artificial or natural phenomena? However, they are not materializations, by any means, but refracted prismatic rays of light, images that Kotter took using a traditional photographic camera. Here, the viewer is confronted by his own conditioning: in the digital age he expects a computer-based formal language, but ultimately this process emerges as consistently analog, or manual. Such a media-critical conception – quite literally – that sets the analog against the digital is also revealed in the meanwhile long-sustained conflict between painting and photography. For despite all their technical perfection, some artifacts give the impression that Kotter is referring to painting with his use of sweeping forms. Thus the artist reopens a long-smouldering dispute regarding ascendancy among the artistic genres: in an almost exemplary fashion, the conflict between photography and painting raises the issue of which medium best meets the claim to truth: painting with its great affinity to philosophy, endorsed for centuries, or photography, which provides documentation of reality via a physical-chemical and so incorruptible process. Kotter leaves it to the viewer to answer this indirectly posed question. His own pictorial works point simultaneously to photography, the new media, and to painting, so that the viewer begins to brood upon the questionability of his own perception, making the credibility and evaluation of each medium into the theme of the works.

Another difficult factor is that Kotter works with and through light: in these, as in other works from the series 'Replaced' (2009-2011), light is used as a means of expression. Looking at the history of light-art in the broadest sense, painted light has been understood both as a purely physical and as a philosophical dimension. This basic assumption, which allows the appearance of both profane and sacred light, is still retained today, although slide and video projection, the technology of the new media, photography and film are now represented alongside painting. Sometimes light is employed as a simple dramatic aid in images and installations, and sometimes it is a carrier of meaning; its themes including technological utopias, anthropologies, media-oriented epistemology, culture-critical and social scientific perspectives associated with names like Robert Delaunay, László Moholy-Nagy, Dan Flavin, Bruce Nauman, James Turrell or Mischa Kuball. This brief historical sketch is reflected not only in Kotter's media-critical color photographs, but also in his light installations: Kotter arranges a row of light boxes of the same and differing formats as if on a rehearsal stage, usually located in a monochrome context in the corner of a room. They are found objects, which – thrown away from industrial sites or offices – are given a new meaning. Like a palimpsest, on the one hand the light objects refer to their original usages, for example when their forms are reminiscent of lighting in manufacturing halls and can be seen, therefore, as a warning reminder of industrial production's alienating work atmosphere; on the other hand, they indicate something new, providing messages – new or long-concealed – in the field of art. Deputizing, almost, for what is hoped for but never achieved in social and cultural fields, it seems that these objects succeed in liberating us from the constraints of social responsibility. Kotter offers the viewer such a dimension of his works – i.e. critical, self-reflective and oriented on insight, and in the same breath he re-conjures the elementary utopias of modernism.

KAI-UWE HEMKEN

THE WORKS

TUNNEL VIEW "DOWN UNDER"

2011

Plexiglas, mirror, metal, color-changing LED lights, and remote control

31 1/2 x 31 1/2 x 6 1/2 in

80 x 80 x 17 cm

Edition 3+2 AP

Museum Ritter, Germany (Permanent Collection)

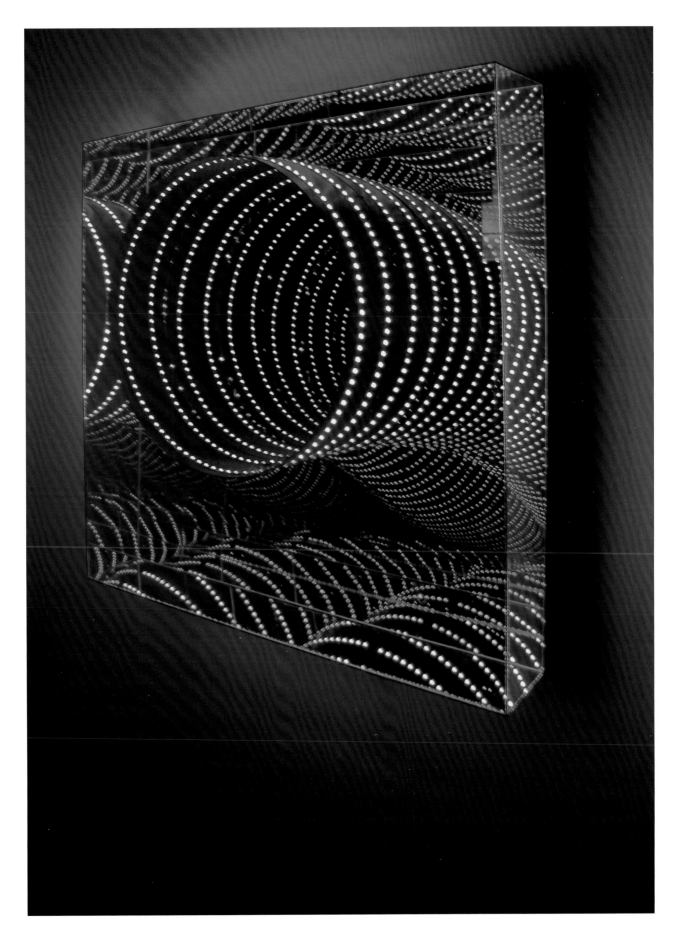

Studio d'Arte Contemporanea di Pino Casagrande, Rome

REPLACED

2009

polished stainless steel light box, 3 aluminum light boxes, perforated metal, aluminum plate, contact breaker,

Plexiglas, and wall paint

Variable Dimensions

CLIFFS (ORANGE)

2010

laserchrome on dibond with Diasec face

47 1/4 x 35 1/2 in

120 x 90 cm

Edition: 3+1 AP

REPLACED

2009

3 aluminum light boxes, stainless steel, contact breaker, Plexiglas, and wall paint

Variable Dimensions

TUNNEL VIEW "DOWN UNDER"

2011

Plexiglas, mirror, metal, color-changing LED lights, and remote control

31 1/2 x 31 1/2 x 6 1/2 in

80 x 80 x 17 cm

Edition 3+2 AP

TWIN

2011

slide on Plexiglas, chrome, color-changing LED lights, and remote control

78 3/4 x 11 4/5 x 3 1/6 inches, each

200 x 30 x 8 cm, each

COLOUR GRADIENT + REPLACED

2009

wooden boxes, Plexiglas, contact breaker, aluminum light boxes, aluminum plate, neon lights, and wall paint

Variable Dimensions

Galerie Michaela Stock, Vienna

CHROMATIC LIGHT BLOCK

2010

slide in Plexiglas and LED lights

23 2/3 x 23 2/3 x 6 in

60 x 60 x 15 cm

TUBE

2011

wood, metal, Plexiglas, mirror, color-changing LED lights, and remote control

63 x 23 2/3 x 23 2/3 in

160 x 60 x 60 cm

Edition: 3+2 AP

REPLACED

2009

neon lights, contact breaker, and wall paint

Variable Dimensions

TWIN

2011

slide on Plexiglas, chrome, color-changing LED lights, and remote control

78 3/4 x 11 4/5 x 3 1/6 inches, each

200 x 30 x 8 cm, each

TWIN

2010

slide on Plexiglas, chrome, color-changing LED lights, and remote control

78 3/4 x 11 4/5 x 3 1/6 inches, each

200 x 30 x 8 cm, each

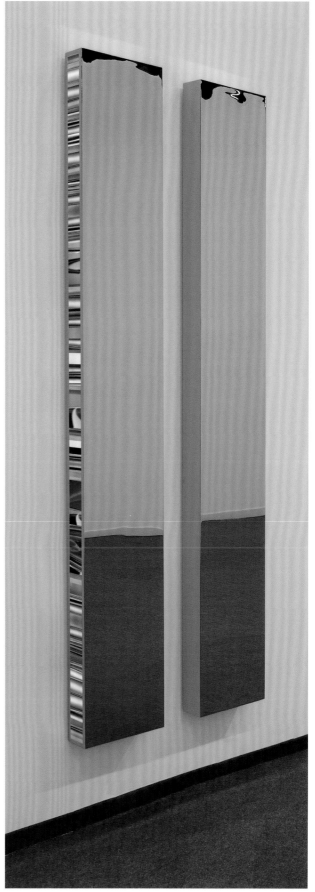

TWIN

2010

slide on Plexiglas, Corten steel, color-changing LED lights, and remote control

78 3/4 x 7 7/8 x 3 1/6 inches, each

200 x 20 x 8 cm, each

Studio d'Arte Contemporanea di Pino Casagrande, Rome

CLIFFS (GRAY)

2010

laserchrome on dibond with Diasec face

47 1/4 x 35 1/2 in

120 x 90 cm

Edition: 3+1 AP

BALANCE

2008

Electro foil and Inverter

Variable Dimensions

Shunt – London Bridge with Kinetica Museum London (Permanent Collection)

TUNNEL VIEW "DOWN UNDER"

2010

Plexiglas, mirror, metal, color-changing LED lights, and remote control

39 1/3 x 39 1/3 x 6 1/2 in

100 x 100 x 17 cm

Edition: 1+1 AP

TWIN

2010

slide on Plexiglas, Corten steel, color-changing LED lights, and remote control

78 3/4 x 7 7/8 x 3 1/6 inches, each

200 x 20 x 8 cm, each

REPLACED

2011

12 aluminum light boxes, contact breaker, and Plexiglas

Variable Dimensions

Stadtgalerie Klagenfurt, Austria

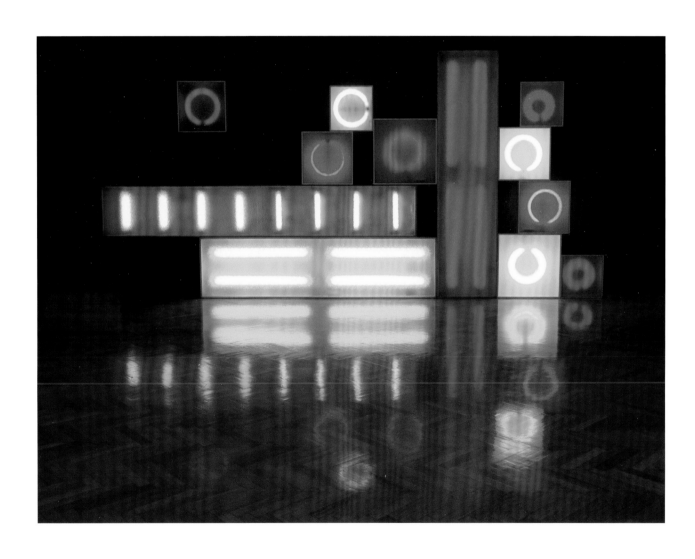

BIOGRAPHY

1966	Born in Muhldorf am Inn, Germany
1993- 1994	Art Students League, New York
2001 - 2003	MediaDesign Akademie Munich, Germany
2004	Culture award, E-ON Bavaria, Germany
2011	Artist in Residence, Art Radionica Lazareti, Dubrovnik, Croatia
Since 2007	Lecturer at State Academy of Art and Design Stuttgart, Germany

Currently lives and works in Berlin.

SELECTED SOLO EXHIBITIONS

2011	*Light Sensitive*, De Buck Gallery, New York
	Patrick Heide Contemporary Art, London
	Point of View, Priveekollektie, Heusden, Netherlands
	Deflection, Studio d'Arte Contemporanea Pino Casagrande, Rome
2010	*Transformation*, Priveekollektie, Heusden, Netherlands
2009	Gallery Michaela Stock, Vienna,
	Replaced, Patrick Heide Contemporary Art London
2008	*The Very Best...*, Gallery Benden & Klimczak, Cologne
	Balance, Shunt London, with Kinetica Museum, London
	Colour Rush, Gallery Bernd Lausberg, Toronto
2007	*Colour Rush and Blue Line*, Patrick Heide Contemporary Art, London
2006	*Light Colour Room*, Gallery Bernd Lausberg, Düsseldorf
2005	*Chromatic Impulse*, Berlinische Galerie with Spectral, Germany
2004	*Balance*, Raum für Kunst, Kunstverein Ravensburg, Germany
	Illuminations, Aedes Berlin, Germany
	Macro Landscape, Patrick Heide Contemporary Art, London
2003	*Lichtecht*, Patrick Heide Contemporary Art, London
2002	*Light and Colour*, Bezirks Galerie, Bezirk Oberbayern, Munich
	Beauty in Plastic, Stadtmuseum Neuötting, Germany
2001	*Blue Line*, Pasinger Fabrik, Munich
2000	*Landscape in Plastic*, Gallery Hofmeisterhaus, Massing/Rottal, Germany
1999	*Stilleben*, Gallery Benden & Klimczak, Cologne
1998	*Spurensicherung*, Haus der Kultur, Waldkraiburg, Germany
	Death Culture in the Chapel, Castle-Klebing, Germany
1997	*Diary with Sound Collage*, Modern Theatre Munich, Germany
	Gallery Notwehr, Munich
1996	*Memory*, ARTgerecht, Hamburg
1994	*Body Language*, Radiocenter of Bratislava, Slovakia
1993	*Talk to Me*, Galerie & Atelier, Vienna
1992	Stadtmuseum Waldkraiburg, Germany
	Daydreams, Chuck Levitan Gallery, New York

SELECTED GROUP EXHIBITIONS

2011	*Story for Reflection*, Gallery Michaela Stock, Vienna
	New Works, Bestregarts, Frankfurt
	Summer Selections, De Buck Gallery, New York
	Patrick Heide Contemporary Art, London
	Art Radionica Lazareti, Dubrovnik, Croatia
	Sensitive Extra, Museum of Contemporary Art, Zagreb, Croatia
	Deflection, Gallery Viltin, Budapest, Hungary
	Click Clique, Lausberg Contemporary, Toronto
	Konkrete Abstraction, Lausberg Contemporary, Düsseldorf
	Winter Thaw, Lausberg Contemporary, Toronto
2010	*Dialog*, Gallery Grazia Blumberg, Recklinghausen, Germany
	Summer Show, Lausberg Contemporary, Toronto
	Beyod Painting, Lausberg Contemporary, Toronto
2009	*Best of Lausberg Contemporary*, Lausberg Contemporary, Toronto
	Trilogie: Berlin – London – Rome, ArtMbassy Berlin
2008	*Best Before*, Stadtgalerie Klagenfurt, Germany
	Infected, Priveekollektie, Holland
	German Photography Today, bkhf Gallery Miami, FL
2007	*Preview 2008*, Gallery Benden & Klimczak, Cologne
	Obsession with Technics, ArtMbassy Berlin, Germany
	Suitcase, Istituto Italiano di Cultura, Cologne
	In the Flux, Kinetica Museum, London
	Best Before..., Kunstverein Aschaffenburg, Germany
2006	*Life Forms*, Kinetica Museum, London
	Fire and Ice, Rosenbaum Contemporary, Boca Raton, FL
2005	*Reflections*, Gallery Kashya Hildebrand, Geneva
	Rot als Farbe, Gallery Bernd Lausberg, Düsseldorf
	Spectrum, Gallery Kashya Hildebrand, New York
	Look!, Berlinerkunst Project, NY Arts Magazine, Berlin
	Solaris, Gallery Kashya Hildebrand, Zurich
2003	*Lichtung II*, Backfabrik, Berlin
	Patrick Heide Contemporary Art, London
	Illuminationen, BerlinerKunstprojekt Annex, Berlin
2001	*Kraft und Magie*, Oberbayerische Kulturtage Altötting, Germany

2000	*Kulturmodell Passau*, Germany
	Grosse Kunstaustellung, Haus der Kunst, Munich
	Städtische Galerie im Park, Viersen, Germany
1999	*I Love You*, Kultur Forum Oberalteich, Germany
	The Museum as Muse: Artists Reflect, Museum of Modern Art, New York
	01, Keio University, Tokyo
1998	*Country Without Borders*, Abraham Lubelski Gallery, New York
	Neue Galerie Oberhausmuseum, Passau, Germany
1997	*Keine Erinnerung*, Old Tax Office, Rosenheim, Germany
	Metamorphosia, Kultur Modell Passau, Germany
1996	*Haus der Kultur*, Waldkraiburg, Germany
	Sonic Identity, 450 Broadway Gallery, New York
1995	*Gallery Hofmeisterhaus*, Massing/Rottal, Germany
1994	*Annual Art Exhibition*, Stadtmuseum Waldkraiburg, Germany
	Cyber Culture, Dariusz Gubala Gallery, New York
	Castle-Schloßhof, Austria
1993	*Vertigo Art*, Dariusz Gubala Gallery, New York
	Madelyn Jordon Gallery, New York

© De Buck Gallery 2011

De Buck Gallery
511 W 25Th Street , Suite 502
New York, NY 10001
T. +1 212 255 5735
E. info@debuckgallery.com
www.debuckgallery.com

Lay-out and typesetting

Stipontwerpt, Antwerp, Belgium
www.stipontwerpt.be

Printer

Daneels Graphic Group, Beerse, Belgium
www.daneels.be

ISBN 978 0 615 54435 9

Photo Credits

Photographs courtesy of Hans Kotter
Cover image, p13, p21, p31, p37 courtesy of Ottavio Celestino

Essay

Annett Zinsmeister

Annett Zinsmeister is an artist and author, and Professor for Visual Arts
and Experimental Design at State Academy of Fine Arts in Stuttgart. She
lives in Berlin. More information: www.annett-zinsmeister.de

Kai-Uwe Hemken *translated by Lucinda Rennison*

Kai-Uwe Hemken is an art historian and Professor for Art Science at
the School of Art and Design Kassel, Germany. He also curated several
exhibitions about modern art at the K20 in Düsseldorf, New Museum
Weimar, Sprengel Museum Hanover, Van Abbemuseum Eindhoven and
others. He lives in Bochum, Germany.
More information: www.kunsthochschule-kassel.de